WARS THAT CHANGED AMERICAN HISTORY

The Mexican-American War

By Matthew Kachur and Jon Sterngass

WORLD ALMANAC® LIBRARY

Please visit our Web site at: www.www.garethstevens.com
For a free color catalog describing World Almanac® Library's list of high-quality books
and multimedia programs, call 1-800-848-2928 (USA) or 1-800-387-3178 (Canada).
World Almanac® Library's fax: (414) 332-3567

Library of Congress Catalog-in-Publication Data

Kachur, Matthew, 1960-
  The Mexican-American War / by Matthew Kachur and John Sterngass. — North American ed.
    p. cm. — (Wars that changed American history)
  Includes bibliographical references and index.
  ISBN-10: 0-8368-7290-8 – ISBN-13: 978-0-8368-7290-3 (lib. bdg.)
  ISBN-10: 0-8368-7299-1 – ISBN-13: 978-0-8368-7299-6 (softcover)
  1. Mexican War, 1846-1848—Juvenile literature. I. Sterngass, Jon.
II. Title. III. Series
  E404.K33   2007
  973.6'2—dc22   2006011837

First published in 2007 by
World Almanac® Library
A Member of the WRC Media Family of Companies
330 West Olive Street, Suite 100
Milwaukee, WI 53212 USA

Copyright © 2007 by World Almanac® Library.

A Creative Media Applications, Inc. Production
Writers: Matthew Kachur and Jon Sterngass
Design and Production: Alan Barnett, Inc.
Editor: Susan Madoff
Copy Editor: Laurie Lieb
Proofreader: Tania Bissell
Indexer: Nara Wood
World Almanac® Library editorial direction: Mark J. Sachner
World Almanac® Library editor: Leifa Butrick
World Almanac® Library art direction: Tammy West
World Almanac® Library production: Jessica Morris

Picture credits: The Library of Congress: pages 5, 18, 37, 40, 43; The Center for American History, The University of Texas
at Austin: pages 6, 13; The Granger Collection: cover and pages 7, 10, 29; New York Public Library, Astor, Lenox, and
Tilden Foundations: pages 11, 31, 33, 42; Northwind Pictures Archives: pages 15, 23, 24, 25, 32, 38; Texas State Library
and Archives Commission: page 17; Courtesy of the State Preservation Board, Austin, Texas: page 20; Picture History: page
28; Getty Images: page 36; Associated Press: page 41; Map courtesy of Ortelius Design.

Printed in the United States of America

1 2 3 4 5 6 7 8 9 10 09 08 07 06

Table of Contents

Cover: After three days of fighting and fierce resistance from the Mexican army, U.S. troops were successful in capturing the fortress town of Monterrey, Mexico. The battle, fought from September 21–23, 1846, resulted in staggering losses for the U.S. Army.

INTRODUCTION

From the time when America declared its independence in the 1700s to the present, every war in which Americans have fought has been a turning point in the nation's history. All of the major wars of American history have been bloody, and all of them have brought tragic loss of life. Some of them have been credited with great results, while others partly or entirely failed to achieve their goals. Some of them were widely supported; others were controversial and exposed deep divisions within the American people. None will ever be forgotten.

The American Revolution created a new type of nation based on the idea that the government should serve the people. As a result of the Mexican-American War, the young country expanded dramatically. Controversy over slavery in the new territory stoked the broader controversy between Northern and Southern states over the slavery issue and powers of state governments versus the federal government. When the slave states seceded, President Abraham Lincoln led the Union into a war against the Confederacy—the Civil War—that reunited a divided nation and ended slavery.

▼ Wars have shaped the history of the United States of America since the nation was founded in 1776. Conflict in this millennium continues to alter the decisions the government makes and the role the United States plays on the world stage.

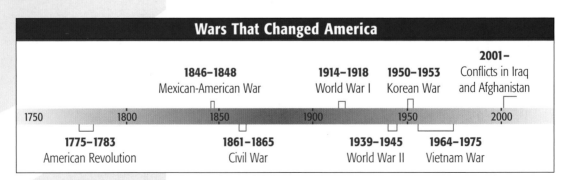

Wars That Changed America

| 1750 | 1800 | 1850 | 1900 | 1950 | 2000 |

1846–1848 Mexican-American War

1914–1918 World War I

1950–1953 Korean War

2001– Conflicts in Iraq and Afghanistan

1775–1783 American Revolution

1861–1865 Civil War

1939–1945 World War II

1964–1975 Vietnam War

The roles that the United States played in World War I and World War II helped transform the country into a major world power. In both these wars, the entry of the United States helped turn the tide of the war.

Later in the twentieth century, the United States engaged in a Cold War rivalry with the Soviet Union. During this time, the United States fought two wars to prevent the spread of communism. The Korean War essentially ended in a stalemate, and after years of combat in the Vietnam War, the United States withdrew. Both claimed great numbers of American lives, and following its defeat in Vietnam, the United States became more cautious in its use of military force.

That trend changed when the United States led the war that drove invading Iraqi forces from Kuwait in 1990. After the al-Qaeda terrorist attacks of September 11, 2001, the United States again led a war, this time against Afghanistan, which was sheltering al-Qaeda. About two years later, the United States led the invasion that toppled Iraq's dictatorship.

In this book, readers will learn how a brash and confident United States took steps to engage in a war designed to expand the nation from coast to coast, and in the process changed the face of it. The Mexican-American War added land to the United States, in addition to a diverse set of people; and although it was originally intended to expand the nation, in the end, its legacy led to the near dissolution of it.

▲ *This theatrical poster printed in 1890 advertises a variety show that recreated the Siege of Vera Cruz during the Mexican-American War. Americans enjoyed entertainment that showcased their feelings of national pride and the promising future of the United States.*

CHAPTER 1

The United States Expands Westward

▼ An advertisement encourages Americans to emigrate to Texas and help battle the Mexican army in the fight for independence. Every settler who agrees to go receives free passage from the city of New Orleans and 800 acres (324 hectares) of land in exchange.

TEXAS
FOREVER!!

The usurper of the South has failed in his efforts to enslave the freemen of Texas.
The wives and daughters of Texas will be saved from the brutality of Mexican soldiers.
Now is the time to emigrate to the Garden of America.
A free passage, and all found, is offered at New Orleans to all applicants. Every settler receives a location of

EIGHT HUNDRED ACRES OF LAND.

On the 23d of February, a force of 1000 Mexicans came in sight of San Antonio, and on the 25th Gen. St. Anna arrived at that place with 2500 more men, and demanded a surrender of the fort held by 150 Texians, and on the refusal, he attempted to storm the fort, twice, with his whole force, but was repelled with the loss of 500 men, and the Americans lost none. Many of his troops, the liberals of Zacatecas, are brought on to Texas in irons and are urged forward with the promise of the women and plunder of Texas.
The Texian forces were marching to relieve St. Antonio, March the 2d. The Government of Texas is supplied with plenty of arms, ammunition, provisions, &c. &c.

The Mexican-American War (1846–1848) changed the face of the United States geographically, culturally, and politically. The war, which resulted in a victory for the United States, increased the size of the country by more than 20 percent. The United States took control of the Mexican provinces of California and New Mexico (which contained the future states of Nevada, Utah, Colorado, Arizona, and New Mexico). The victory completed U.S. expansion across North America to the Pacific Ocean, and the harbors of San Francisco and San Diego opened the door to trade with Asia.

At the same time, Mexico lost 529,017 square miles (1,370,154 square kilometers), more than one-third of its territory. Los Angeles, San Francisco, Albuquerque, Santa Fe, and Salt Lake City, all once in Mexico, became U.S. cities.

The United States' victory, however, caused a major problem. The new land brought the issue of the expansion of slavery to the forefront of U.S. politics. The debate over whether slavery should be allowed in the new territories was a major cause of the Civil War (1861–1865) between the Northern and Southern states.

U.S. Expansion before 1830

European settlers in North America had been moving west ever since they began to settle the East Coast in the 1600s. In the Treaty of Paris (1783) that ended the American Revolution and formally established the United States of America as an independent nation, Britain gave almost all the land from the Atlantic Ocean to the Mississippi River to the United States. The new nation continued to expand. In 1803, the United States bought the Louisiana Territory from France, purchasing 828,000 square miles (2,155,500 sq km) for $15 million. The purchase more than doubled the size of the United States. Still, the country pressed its neighbors for more land. In 1819, the United States wrested control of Florida from Spain.

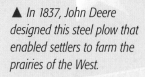

▲ In 1837, John Deere designed this steel plow that enabled settlers to farm the prairies of the West.

Changes in the United States

By the 1840s, almost half of all Americans lived west of the Appalachian Mountains. The Erie Canal, completed in 1825, connected the Great Lakes with the Hudson River. This 363-mile (584-km) **canal** made it easier to ship bulky products such as coal, lumber, and wheat from the Midwest to the East and then to Europe. Railroads, developed in the 1830s, made travel faster than ever. In 1800, a traveler from New York needed a week to reach Pittsburgh. By 1850, one day on a railroad took a New Yorker all the way to Cleveland.

New agricultural inventions also encouraged expansion. In 1831, Cyrus McCormick invented the reaper. By using this machine, farmers could harvest crops more quickly than they did by hand. The time saved allowed them to plant more crops on larger pieces of land. John Deere, a blacksmith in Illinois, made a steel plow in 1837. It was the first plow strong enough to break through the tough prairie soil of the West. As the steel plow and the reaper became popular, they helped drive the desire for new land to farm.

As the country shifted toward large-scale farming and industrialization, people began having larger families, and the population of the United States almost doubled between 1820 and 1840. The rapid population growth, combined with advances in transportation, communication, agriculture, and industry, convinced many Americans that their country was the best place in the world to live. Many people in the growing nation continued to proclaim the need for even more land. In 1840, the most obvious targets for U.S. expansion were nearby territories held by foreign nations, such as Canada (held by Great Britain) and the northern provinces of Mexico.

Manifest Destiny

In 1845, newspaperman John O'Sullivan coined the term *manifest destiny*. In an editorial he wrote for the *Democratic Review*, O'Sullivan said that the manifest, or obvious and inevitable, destiny of the United States was to expand across the continent and that nothing could prevent such an expansion because it was perfectly just and supported by God.

The idea of manifest destiny dominated American thought from 1830 to 1850. Possible U.S. expansion seemed limitless. At times, supporters of manifest destiny campaigned for the United States to take over Canada, Mexico, Caribbean islands, Central America, Brazil, and even Pacific islands as far as Okinawa.

Many Americans viewed manifest destiny as an unselfish attempt to extend liberty. They thought that U.S.-style democracy would follow the U.S. flag into any new lands where Americans moved.

Evils of Manifest Destiny

Many white Americans who talked about manifest destiny believed that people who were not white and not of European descent, including Native Americans and African Americans, were inferior. Conflict with Native Americans began soon after Europeans arrived in the Western Hemisphere. Thousands of Indians were killed and pushed off their land. As soon as Europeans settled the thirteen colonies, they began supporting the slave trade from Africa. By 1840, 2.5 million African Americans lived in slavery in the United States.

The government of the United States did not protect Native Americans or African Americans. In fact, the government helped to illegally remove Native Americans from their land. In 1837, the United States forced fifteen thousand Cherokee (Keetoowha) to leave their homelands in Georgia and move to Oklahoma. An estimated four thousand Indians died on the 1,200-mile (1,930-km) march known as the Trail of Tears.

Most white Americans were proud of the United States. They could, however, also be greedy and racist. Supporters of manifest destiny wanted to expand the West, either by buying the land or by conquering it. Few Americans, however, would say this in so many words. Instead, they claimed that the conquest of the West was a way to extend liberty and progress. They did not want to admit that, for many, it was just a chance to obtain land and make money. Today, it is obvious that the

Our Nation's Future

John O'Sullivan wrote that "it was the nation's manifest destiny to overspread and to possess the whole of the continent which Providence [God] has given us for the development of the great experiment of liberty and… self-government entrusted to us." While never an official policy, manifest destiny combined ideas of U.S. superiority with **nationalism** and **expansionism**.

nineteenth-century idea of manifest destiny caused pain and suffering for many people.

Some Americans in the 1830s and 1840s debated the idea of manifest destiny. They wondered whether it was acceptable to use force to take land belonging to other peoples and countries and add it to the United States. The Mexican-American War served as a test for what Americans believed about their country, manifest destiny, and the place slavery had in their future.

Americans Move to Texas

When Mexico won its independence from Spain in 1821, the new nation was very large. Its northern provinces of Texas, New Mexico, and Upper California were a great distance from Mexico's most populated region around Mexico City. At the time of Mexico's independence, only about twenty-three hundred **Tejanos** (Spanish-speaking residents) lived in Texas.

To encourage people to settle northern Mexico, the Mexican government offered land to any American who would agree to become a Mexican citizen, adopt

The Mexican-American War

the Catholic religion, and bring two hundred families to the area. Those who accepted this arrangement were called empresarios. In 1821, Moses Austin, a land speculator from Missouri, received a land grant that would eventually cover 18,000 acres (7,290 ha). When he died that same year, his son Stephen took over the grant and traveled to Texas to fulfill the terms of his father's agreement. In the next ten years, twenty-five other American settlements were established in east and central Texas.

By 1835, there were more than fifty thousand people living in Mexican Texas: about thirty thousand Anglo-Americans, five thousand black slaves, thirty-five hundred Hispanics, and fourteen thousand Indians. More settlers had moved there in fifteen years than in centuries of Spanish rule. White Americans outnumbered Mexicans in Texas at least eight to one. Most white Americans in Texas never wanted to be part of Mexico. They ignored local laws, practiced slavery, and refused to become Catholics. Many Americans in Texas believed in manifest destiny. They felt that Americans should rule all of North America.

▲ The Mexican army assembles before the Alamo in a fight to take back the fort (and former Spanish mission) that Stephen Austin had captured in one of the early battles for Texan independence.

The Texas Revolt

As more Americans moved to Texas, the Mexican government began to fear, quite rightly, that the Americans would rebel and try to break away from Mexico. In 1835, American settlers staged a revolt in Gonzalez, Texas. They demanded that Mexican troops surrender their cannons. When they failed to do so, the rebels drove the Mexican militia stationed there out of Texas. Stephen Austin attacked San Antonio in December 1835 and conquered the fort known as the

Sam Houston (1793–1863)

Sam Houston moved from Virginia to Tennessee at age thirteen. As a young man, he was curious about Native American culture and spent time with the Cherokee. Houston served in the U.S. Army during the War of 1812 and went on to become a lawyer and serve in the U.S. Congress and then as governor of Tennessee in 1827. Two years later, unhappy after his short marriage failed, he resigned the governorship and moved to Oklahoma to find comfort living among the Cherokee. He became a leader among the Native Americans and served as their **ambassador** to the U.S. government. In 1832, Houston left the Cherokee and traveled to Mexican Texas to seek new opportunity in a land where many American colonists were settling. In the fall of 1835, Houston served as commander of the Texas forces and eventually led the rebels to victory in the Battle of San Jacinto.

Texans elected Houston the first president of the new republic, the first senator from the state of Texas (1845–1859) once it became part of the United States, and then governor. Houston died in 1830. He is the only American who served as governor of two states.

Alamo. Texas declared its independence and quickly adopted a constitution legalizing slavery.

In retaliation, Mexican general Antonio López de Santa Anna approached San Antonio with an army of six thousand soldiers ready to take back the settlement and fort. Fewer than two hundred Texans defended the Alamo. The Mexican **siege** lasted two weeks. In the end, all the Alamo's defenders were killed. Santa Anna went on to defeat the Texans at Goliad, south of San Antonio.

Independence

The American settlers in Texas grew panicky. The Texan army, however, commanded by Sam Houston, turned the tide. In the twenty-minute Battle of San Jacinto (near Houston) on April 21, 1836, the Texans surprised and defeated a larger force of Mexicans. The Mexican army took its afternoon siesta without posting enough guards. While the Mexicans dozed, the Texans attacked, shouting, "Remember the Alamo. Remember Goliad." The Texans suffered fewer than fifty casualties while the Mexicans counted 630 dead.

The Texans captured General Santa Anna at the battle. They forced him to sign a treaty recognizing an independent Texas and set its boundary at the Rio Grande. Then the Texans allowed Santa Anna to return to Mexico. The Mexican congress, however, and later Santa Anna, rejected this treaty. They claimed it was "an agreement carried out under the threat of death." Mexico insisted that Texas was still part of Mexico.

The Lone Star Republic

Texas was now an independent country known as the Republic of Texas. Most Texans, however, wanted to join the United States, the land of their birth. Texan imports and exports went through the U.S. city of New Orleans. Large plantation owners and rich merchants thought that trade would be easier if Texas was part of the United States.

The United States was hesitant to **annex** Texas for two reasons. First, the Mexican government continued to view Texas as a breakaway state that Mexico would one day reconquer. Mexico made it clear that any U.S. attempt to annex Texas would lead to war. Second, Texas was caught up in the national debate over slavery. Most white American settlers in Mexican Texas came from the Southern United States. They were not happy that the Mexican government had made slavery illegal in Texas. Most of these white settlers either owned slaves or hoped to own them someday. When Texas became independent, the new constitution of the Republic of Texas legalized slavery.

Many Northerners, however, did not want Texas to join the United States as a slave state. They believed that Southern slave states already had too much influence over national policy.

Southern political power rested on what was known as the three-fifths compromise. In 1787, the writers of the U.S. Constitution had based the number of members from each state in the House of Representatives on the number of people who lived in each state. Black slaves counted as three-fifths of a person when totaling up the population. Of course, these slaves could not vote and had no freedom. Yet these same slaves added to the white South's political power. The voting power in the House of Representatives was based on population, as were votes in the **Electoral College**, which chose the president. As a result, the slave-holding states had greater representation in the U.S. government than states where slavery was not accepted.

▲ *Sam Houston (pictured here in 1858) led the Texan army to victory at the Battle of San Jacinto. Later he served as the first president of the new republic. The modern cities of Houston and Austin were named for him and Stephen Austin, another respected general in the Texan army.*

In order to be elected or reelected president before 1860, a politician had to appeal heavily to Southern white voters. Of the fifteen presidents before the Civil War, nine were slave-owners. The presidents from the South and three of the others were extremely sympathetic to the South. None of the six presidents from the North was reelected.

American settlers, especially Southerners, continued to flood the Lone Star Republic. In the decade after its independence, the population of Texas soared from 30,000 to 142,000. In 1846, most Texans assumed that somehow they would soon be part of the United States.

Oregon Fever

Americans who believed in manifest destiny did not limit their dreams to Texas and the Southwest. In the Northwest, the Oregon Territory was also a possible target for U.S. expansion. This territory was much larger than the present-day state of Oregon. It included British Columbia in Canada as well as Oregon, Washington, Idaho, and parts of Wyoming and Montana. Fur trapping first brought Americans and Europeans to the Northwest. Since 1818, Great Britain and the United States had jointly occupied the Oregon Territory although neither nation had ever made land treaties with the area's Native Americans.

In the late 1830s, U.S. missionaries sent glowing reports to the government of rich farmland near present-day Portland, Oregon. At the same time, New England merchants became interested in ports on the western coast of North America. In the early 1800s, U.S. ships loaded with anchors, cannon shot, bar iron, sheet copper, candles, and rum were traveling to China and exchanging their cargoes for tea, silks, and lacquerware. The natural harbors at present-day Seattle, Portland, and Vancouver made it easy for Americans to trade with China. From these harbors, merchant ships could sail around Cape Horn at the tip of South America to the eastern coast of the United States.

In 1841, "Oregon fever" broke out. Between 1841 and 1845, the American population of Oregon increased from four hundred to six thousand. Americans were now less willing to share Oregon with Great Britain. A movement began to demand the entire Oregon Territory from Britain as far north as the 54°40' parallel of **latitude**, the border with Russian-owned Alaska. This was an astonishing demand because most Americans had settled south of the forty-ninth parallel. Influenced by the idea of manifest destiny, however, many Americans saw an opportunity to eliminate the British from the west coast of North America.

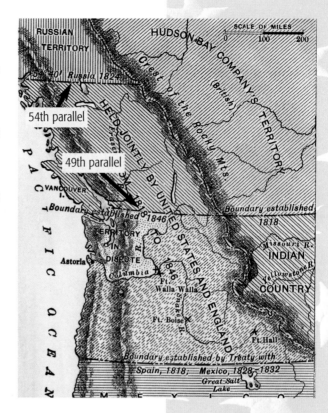

▲ A map of the Oregon Territory illustrates the 54°40' parallel of latitude that became the center of a boundary dispute involving the idea of manifest destiny. Americans believed that they were entitled to take this land from Britain even though few Americans had settled on land any higher than the forty-ninth parallel.

Whigs, Democrats, and the Annexation of Texas

In 1841, President William Henry Harrison died suddenly. Vice president John Tyler, also a Virginian slaveholder, became president. Tyler wanted to be elected president in the next election in 1844, but he needed a popular issue that would appeal to the majority of the nation's voters. Tyler decided to support the annexation of Texas in order to win the votes of the South.

The Whig Party and the Democratic Party were the two major political parties in the United States between 1832 and 1854. Their positions on **social reform** were very different. Almost all American social reformers in this period were **Whigs**. They included **abolitionists** and people who supported women's rights. The Democratic Party usually took a strong proslavery stance. The most outspoken

The presidential election of 1844 was the first time an incumbent, or sitting, president failed to receive the nomination from his party for the subsequent election. John Tyler, who had become president upon William Harrison's death, had alienated the Whigs, and they kicked him out of the party in 1841. Democrats found Tyler untrustworthy and believed he was playing political ping-pong, moving back and forth between the ideals of the two parties.

In the end, the Whigs nominated Henry Clay, a congressional leader who opposed westward expansion, and Democrats chose James Polk, a "dark horse" (virtually unknown and unexpectedly successful) candidate to run for president. Polk broadened the issue of expansion to include the Oregon Territory in addition to Texas. In the end, Clay was forced to weigh in on Texas annexation as well, saying that he would support it if it could be accomplished without bloodshed and on "just and fair" terms.

Although James Polk was virtually unknown before this election, his victory and subsequent presidency effected great change for the United States.

supporters of manifest destiny and expansion by force were usually **Democrats**.

Tyler had been a Whig, but since he became president, he had split from the Whig Party. Northern politicians refused to support Tyler's push to add another slave state to the United States. In 1844, the U.S. Senate voted 35 to 16 against the annexation of Texas.

In the 1844 election, Tyler failed to win the Whig nomination. James Polk, a slaveholding cotton grower and former governor of Tennessee, was elected president. Polk and the Democrats had campaigned on a platform of manifest destiny. They demanded that the United States acquire both Oregon and Texas. The presidential election of 1844 was one of the closest in U.S. history. Polk won by only thirty-eight thousand votes.

The Annexation of Texas

President Tyler claimed that Polk's victory, no matter how close, showed that Americans wanted Texas. Before his term of office concluded, Tyler decided to annex Texas by a joint resolution, which needed only a majority vote in both houses of Congress, instead of a treaty, which required two-thirds approval in the Senate. In February 1845, the U.S. Senate agreed with the House of Representatives by a narrow 27 to 25 margin in approving the annexation of Texas. The annexation of Texas represented the triumph of manifest destiny. As the Whigs feared, it would also lead directly to a war with Mexico. Massachusetts representative (and former president) John Quincy Adams wrote in his diary that the annexation of Texas was the "heaviest calamity that ever befell myself and my country." In the end, the annexation of Texas was one of a series of events leading to the Civil War sixteen years later.

The Mexican-American War

CHAPTER 2

The Mexican-American War Begins

One of John Tyler's last acts as president was to sign the congressional resolution annexing Texas. Tyler then went back to Virginia, leaving James Polk to deal with the consequences. The government of Mexico had stated that there would be a war if the United States annexed Texas. Both Americans and Mexicans waited to see how the new president would deal with that threat.

President Polk believed that the voters had elected him in 1844 to expand the country. American settlers wanted the rich farmland of the Oregon Territory. American merchants wanted the fine harbors and valuable coastal position of California in order to increase their trade with China. In order to do this, Polk had to confront Mexico to the south and Great Britain to the north.

▼ Texas president Anson Jones lowers the flag of the Republic of Texas upon annexation by the United States in 1845.

War Draws Closer

Two days after Polk took office, the Mexican ambassador to the United States filed a protest. He called the annexation of Texas an "act of aggression" and threatened war, but no hostile acts occurred during the rest of 1845. In December 1845, Congress completed the annexation of Texas by approving the admission of Texas to the United States as the twenty-eighth

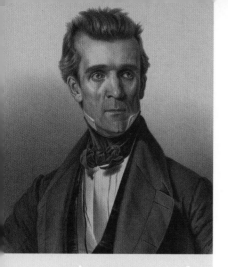

James Polk
(1795–1849)

James Polk, pictured above, was born in North Carolina. His family moved by covered wagon to Tennessee when he was ten. The Polk family prospered and, by 1820, owned thousands of acres and more than fifty slaves. In 1825, Polk was elected to the House of Representatives to represent Tennessee. He rose to power and fame in Congress and was a strong supporter of President Andrew Jackson during his terms in office from 1829 to 1837. Polk's political career seemed to be over, however, when he lost elections for governor of Tennessee in 1841 and 1843. He did, however, win the Democratic presidential nomination in 1844 and the extremely close election. Polk's presidency led directly to the Mexican-American War and the U.S. takeover of the future states of California, Arizona, New Mexico, Utah, Oregon, and Washington.

state and the fifteenth slave state. Polk sent a representative to Mexico with instructions to buy California and New Mexico from the Mexican government for as much as $30 million. The Mexicans refused to meet with him. The Mexican government did not want to give up more of its territory for any amount of money.

"Fifty-four Forty or Fight!"

In 1844, Polk's Northern followers had campaigned enthusiastically to take the whole Oregon Territory in the name of manifest destiny. Northern Democrats shouted the slogan "Fifty-four Forty or Fight!" Those numbers represented the farthest northern border of the Oregon Territory, all the way to the southern border of what was then Russian Alaska. The United States, however, had only the shakiest claim to land as far north as 54°40'.

Great Britain's own claim to Oregon extended to the Columbia River (which now separates the states of Oregon and Washington). There were, however, fewer than one thousand British subjects in the area. British interest in Oregon was fading. The fur trade was dying out. New opportunities in other British colonies, such as New Zealand, lured British settlers away from the Pacific Northwest. British army experts reported that Oregon could not be defended in case of war. Yet as long as the British were in Canada, they were unwilling to give up the possibility of owning ports on the Pacific Ocean. Great Britain had colonies in Asia and wanted to trade goods from North America to China and India.

A Free Hand with Mexico

In December 1845, Polk warned that the British in the Northwest should not interfere with areas that the United States wanted to annex. President Polk,

The Mexican-American War

however, was interested in a peaceful negotiation with Great Britain, especially since war against Mexico looked more likely every day. Polk was willing to compromise. In 1846, the British suggested a boundary at the forty-ninth parallel of latitude from the Strait of Georgia (the channel that separates Vancouver Island from the Canadian mainland and that is part of the inland passage to Alaska) out to the sea. This boundary split the Oregon Territory roughly in half. (See map on page 15.)

On June 15, 1846, the U.S. Senate ratified the Oregon Compromise treaty. The United States acquired the natural harbor at Puget Sound (present-day Seattle), and the British received the harbor at Vancouver as well as Vancouver Island, thereby ensuring that both nations gained ports on the Pacific and good opportunities to trade with Asia. The treaty equally divided the other 500,000 square miles (1,295,000 sq km) of the territory between the United States and Great Britain. The United States acquired the future states of Oregon, Washington, and Idaho and parts of Wyoming and Montana. The British added British Columbia to Canada.

The settlement in Oregon had an enormous indirect effect on U.S. relations with Mexico. The United States, freed of the threat of war in the Northwest, was now able to concentrate its efforts on a military buildup in Texas. "We can now thrash Mexico into decency at our leisure," observed the *New York Herald*.

"Hostilities May Be Considered to Have Commenced"

Although Polk avoided war with Great Britain in Oregon, he encouraged war against Mexico. Polk argued that the Rio Grande was the southern border

Polk's Warning to Mexico

In his first speech as president, Polk insisted that Mexico had no say in U.S. relations with Texas. He said, "I regard the question of annexation [of Texas] belonging exclusively to the United States and Texas. They are independent powers…and foreign nations have no right to interfere with them or to take exception to their reunion."

Fast Fact

When President Polk received the Oregon treaty from the British, he took the unusual step of giving it directly to the Senate without supporting or rejecting it. By doing this, Polk tried to avoid criticism that he had "surrendered" half of Oregon from people who had campaigned for him under the slogan "Fifty-four Forty or Fight."

of Texas—a controversial claim. In 1816, the Spanish government had set the southern border of Texas at the Nueces River, 130 miles (209 km) northeast of the Rio Grande. The United States had agreed to this boundary in an 1819 treaty that allowed the United States to purchase Florida in exchange for giving up claims to Texas. The Mexican government had never changed this boundary. When Texans captured General Santa Anna at the Battle of San Jacinto in 1836, he agreed that Texas could extend its boundary to the Rio Grande. The Mexican congress, the treaty-making body under the Mexican constitution, immediately rejected the agreement. In the ten years after 1836, Texas had not settled the area below the Nueces, and the Rio Grande was never actually under Texan control. With the annexation of Texas in 1845, however, the United States adopted Texas's position and claimed the Rio Grande as the new border.

In June 1845, President Polk sent twenty-three hundred troops into the disputed area between the Rio

▼ *Mexican general Santa Anna (lying injured on the ground) surrenders to General Sam Houston at the Battle of San Jacinto on April 21, 1836. The outnumbered Texan army surprised and defeated the Mexican troops while they lay resting.*

Grande and the Nueces River. In January 1846, Polk ordered General Zachary Taylor to advance to the Corpus Christi area and establish a fort south of the Nueces. The fort, at present-day Point Isabel, stands at the mouth of the Rio Grande directly across from the Mexican city of Matamoros. Polk warned Taylor not to begin fighting, but he also told the general to consider any Mexican crossing of the Rio Grande an act of war.

The Mexicans viewed Taylor's actions as an act of war and sent their own soldiers to the area. On April 24, 1846, a clash occurred when Mariano Arista, the commander of the Mexican Army of the North, ordered his soldiers across the Rio Grande. "Hostilities may

The Mexican-American War

be considered to have commenced," Taylor wrote to Polk. On May 8, the American army of twenty-three hundred men defeated a Mexican force of thirty-four hundred at Palo Alto on disputed ground about 5 miles (8 km) from present-day Brownsville, Texas. The next day, the Americans routed four thousand Mexicans at nearby Resaca de la Palma. Fewer than fifty U.S. soldiers lost their lives in these engagements while Mexican casualties numbered more than one thousand.

This was a surprising result. Most neutral observers had assumed that Mexico's larger army would defeat the U.S. forces. Mexican troops, however, were positioned poorly and did not work well as a unit. There was constant infighting among Mexican political leaders, their army officers, and the troops. In addition, U.S. artillery (cannons) was very effective in canceling out the Mexican advantage in number of soldiers.

The U.S. Declaration of War

President Polk had already decided to go to war with Mexico before any fighting broke out. He had written several drafts of a declaration of war against Mexico. He kept them in his desk, however, because he had no excuse to go to war that would win the support of the American people. When Taylor's report reached Washington, D.C., Polk excitedly changed his war message to reflect the fighting along the border. These first acts of violence allowed him to justify the war against Mexico and rally American patriotism.

On May 11, the president asked Congress to declare war against Mexico. He claimed, "Mexico

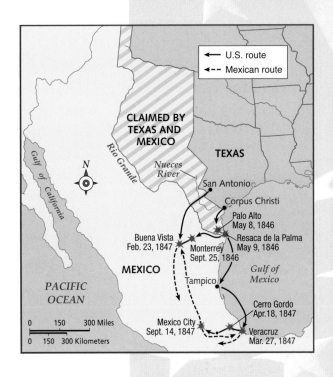

▲ This map shows the location of the Nueces River and the new boundary between Texas and Mexico at the Rio Grande, as declared by President Polk. The boundary dispute, which became the justification Polk needed to start a war, led to battles throughout Mexico, from Corpus Christi south to Mexico City. The map also shows the land gained by the United States in its victory, including New Mexico and part of California.

Abraham Lincoln and the War

The voters of southern Illinois elected the thirty-eight-year-old Abraham Lincoln to the U.S. House of Representatives in 1846. As a member of the Whig Party, Lincoln opposed the war against Mexico. Lincoln voted for a resolution that declared the war unnecessary. In 1847, Lincoln introduced the "Spot Resolution" in Congress, demanding that President Polk identify the exact spot where Mexicans had supposedly invaded United States territory. His point was that the territory belonged to Mexico. He said, "That soil was not ours."

As late as 1848, Lincoln compared President Polk's speeches to "the half insane mumbling of a fever-dream." Lincoln's opposition to the war was unpopular in southern Illinois and he was not chosen to run for Congress again.

has passed the boundary of the United States, has invaded our territory and shed American blood upon American soil.... War exists, and, notwithstanding all our efforts to avoid it, exists by act of Mexico." On May 13, 1846, the Senate voted 40 to 2 to declare war on Mexico. The House of Representatives agreed by a 174 to 14 vote.

The Wilmot Proviso

One hot summer day in August 1846, David Wilmot, a Democratic U.S. representative from Pennsylvania, rose from his seat in Congress. He wanted to add a short **proviso** to a bill in Congress supporting the Mexican-American War. The Wilmot Proviso stated simply that none of the territory gained from Mexico should be open to slavery: "Provided, that as an express and fundamental condition to the acquisition of any territory from the Republic of Mexico by the United States...neither slavery nor involuntary servitude shall ever exist in any part of said territory."

David Wilmot did not particularly want to abolish slavery, nor did he care about the plight of enslaved African Americans. Instead, Wilmot claimed to be defending the rights of white people. Like many Northerners, Wilmot opposed slavery in the West only because it would limit the job opportunities for Northern free whites. The Wilmot Proviso twice passed the U.S. House of Representatives, but the Southern-dominated Senate never approved it. The Wilmot Proviso, however, turned the expansion of slavery into the most important national discussion in the United States at that time.

President Polk had no deep feelings about slavery one way or another. Polk wrote in his diary that the Wilmot Proviso was "a mischievous and foolish amendment.... What connection slavery had with making peace with Mexico it is difficult to conceive." President Polk was very wrong in this assumption.

The Mexican View of the War

The Mexicans viewed the cause of the war with the United States somewhat differently from their American opponents. Mexico claimed that the U.S. annexation of Texas was illegal because Texas was a province that illegally broke away from Mexico. To Mexico, the U.S. claim that the Rio Grande was the southern boundary of Texas was meaningless because the border had been the Nueces River for hundreds of years. Mexicans believed that the entire crisis was simply a way for the United States to seize even more Mexican territory that had nothing to do with Texas. In Mexico, the war appeared as an act of robbery by an overly aggressive nation.

Some Mexicans looked forward to a war. Mexico took great pride in its own military tradition. The nation had won its own revolution against Spain twenty-five years earlier. The Mexican army, which contained about thirty-two thousand soldiers, was more than four times the size of the original U.S. force. Mexico did not realize that a call for volunteers would swell the U.S. Army to more than one hundred thousand men.

Mexican troops also had more military experience than the U.S. Army, which had not fought a war since the War of 1812 against Great Britain. In late 1845, a new Mexican government came to power led by Mariano Parades y Arrillaga. This government pledged to maintain national honor and protect valuable lands from Mexico's northern neighbor.

▲ A hand-colored woodcut illustrates Mexican troops getting ready for battle in 1850. The Mexican army, although large in number, was disorganized as a result of political disagreements within the country.

CHAPTER 3

The Lure of California

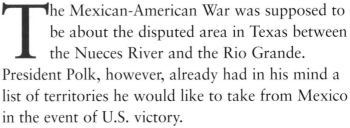

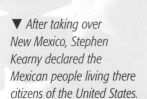

▼ *After taking over New Mexico, Stephen Kearny declared the Mexican people living there citizens of the United States.*

The Mexican-American War was supposed to be about the disputed area in Texas between the Nueces River and the Rio Grande. President Polk, however, already had in his mind a list of territories he would like to take from Mexico in the event of U.S. victory.

The largest Mexican settlement west of the Mississippi was the city of Santa Fe. After Mexico won its independence in 1821, American traders were welcomed in Santa Fe. These merchants carried manufactured goods from Missouri on the bumpy, 800-mile (1,287-km) dirt path known as the Santa Fe Trail. About sixty thousand Mexicans lived in New Mexico.

When the Mexican-American War began in June 1846, Stephen Kearny, a thirty-year career officer in the U.S. Army, marched 1,000 miles (1,600 km) from Kansas to New Mexico. He had seventeen hundred men and orders to occupy Mexico's northern provinces of New Mexico and California. In August, without any Mexican troops in the region to defend Santa Fe, Kearny's Army of the West took the settlement without a shot. Leaving troops in the region to keep order, Kearny set off for California.

Soon after Kearny's departure, revolts broke out around the settlement. The largest uprising, known as the Taos Revolt, took place in January 1847. In February 1847, U.S. forces put down the rebellion and took complete control of New Mexico.

"The Texas Game"

In 1827, only about four thousand Mexicans of Spanish origin lived in California. They were called **Californios**. In the 1830s, the Mexican government passed laws allowing it to take the land that belonged to the Catholic missions (established years earlier by Spain) in California. The government divided this land into huge pieces and sold it or gave it away. By the time of the Mexican-American War, about eight hundred land grants had been made, totaling 9 million acres (3.65 million ha). More than fifteen hundred Americans moved to Mexican California in the following years, drawn by the opportunity to own this valuable land. Although some Californios created great ranching empires, most were poor ranch hands who took care of the cattle for the American and Mexican landholders. There were also thirty thousand Native Americans living in the region who were treated almost like slaves by the ranchers.

Like the American settlers in Texas, the Americans in California had no loyalty to Mexico. One American resident correctly predicted that the "American population will soon be sufficiently numerous to play the Texas game." He meant that there would soon be more Americans than Mexicans in California. Then they would rebel against Mexico and demand to be part of the United States.

The Bear Flag Republic

President Polk's desire to make California a part of the United States reached its peak in the mid-1840s. As Stephen Kearny traveled westward, Polk sent

▼ The flag of the Bear Flag Republic represents the region of California freed from Mexico by John Frémont.

secret orders to the commander of the U.S. Navy in the Pacific to seize San Francisco, a port in northern California, if war broke out between the United States and Mexico.

When Kearny's force reached California in September 1846, he found the province already free from Mexico. American explorer John Frémont and a few hundred Americans in the Sacramento area of northern California had organized a rebellion even before news of the war had reached California. With almost no Mexicans in the area to resist, the rebels declared themselves the Bear Flag Republic, named after the strongest animal in the region. The Bear Flag Republic lasted only about a month. Once word of it reached the U.S. government, the U.S. Navy landed 250 sailors and marines in Monterey, the Mexican capital of California, located south of San Francisco. They took the city and declared California a part of the United States.

Kearny's troops then turned southward in order to conquer the rest of the province. In southern California, Mexicans drove the Americans from Los Angeles, but reinforcements from Kearny turned the tide. By January 1847, U.S. forces had captured the Mexican fortified towns of San Francisco, Monterey, Santa Barbara, Los Angeles, and San Diego. The entire province of California was now in U.S. hands.

Turmoil in Mexico

In the summer of 1846, Zachary Taylor's army on the Rio Grande had swelled to twenty thousand men, mostly volunteers. There were no battles at that time, however, because the Mexican government was collapsing. Rather than uniting the Mexicans, the U.S. invasion had divided Mexico into two opposing sides. In northern Mexico, some citizens actually

The Mexican-American War

worked with the U.S. Army to overthrow the central government. The Mexican defeats at Palo Alto and Resaca de la Palma led to a revolt by many soldiers throughout Mexico. The country was in complete turmoil bordering on civil war.

Between June 1844 and September 1847, Mexico had six different presidents. Almost all came to power because of a popular or military uprising against the previous president. Several Mexican provinces refused to cooperate with the central government in the fight against the United States.

The Return of Santa Anna

Antonio López de Santa Anna was the most important Mexican leader in the period from 1820 to 1860. He was in and out of power several times. In 1846, he was living on the Caribbean island of Cuba, having been exiled from Mexico one year earlier.

With California, New Mexico, and Texas in American hands, President Polk was looking for a way to end the war. From Cuba, Santa Anna negotiated with the United States. He promised to work for a truce if he could return to Mexico. The United States decided to help Santa Anna return to Mexico by allowing him to pass through a U.S. naval blockade positioned off the coast of Mexico. He arrived in Vera Cruz in August 1846. Once in Mexico, however, Santa Anna went back on his word to the United States and refused to sign any peace treaty that gave away Mexican territory. Santa Anna's enormous popularity made him the only Mexican leader who had a chance of reuniting Mexico. The Mexican government gave him command of its army. In December 1846, he was elected president by the Mexican congress. He quickly gathered an army of almost twenty thousand men to try to stop Zachary Taylor's advance.

The Volunteers Take the Field

Most U.S. soldiers in the Mexican-American War were volunteers. Regular army officers constantly complained that the volunteers lacked discipline and thought only of the glory of battle. One officer complained that "the volunteers will scarcely work; daily life was not embraced in their conception of the war." An officer of the First Mississippi Regiment wrote, "One who has never commanded a company of volunteers [sic] can form no idea of the unpleasantness of the life.... Voluntiers I am satisfied will never do for an invading army." Nonetheless, the volunteers generally performed no better or worse than the regular army, with one exception. The Battle of Buena Vista was fought almost entirely by volunteers on the American side.

The Battle of Buena Vista

In September 1846, the Mexican army on the Texas border had retreated across the Rio Grande. Zachary Taylor decided to pursue it. After a five-day battle,

▲ *Zachary Taylor defeated the Mexican army at the Battle of Buena Vista. The Mexican troops were confused by smoke from gunfire on the battlefield. After intense fighting, the army withdrew from the area, leaving the Americans in control of northern Mexico for the remainder of the war.*

the Americans occupied Monterrey, the major city of northern Mexico. In January 1847, Santa Anna moved north with about twenty thousand troops. He had learned that many of Taylor's soldiers were being withdrawn to take part in General Winfield Scott's invasion of Mexico at Vera Cruz, the country's major port on the Gulf of Mexico. Taylor's army seemed to be in trouble. It was far from home and outnumbered by the Mexicans by about three to one.

Nonetheless, Taylor refused to retreat and instead took up a defensive position at Buena Vista, not far from Monterrey. When Santa Anna attacked at Buena Vista on February 22, 1847, the fighting was extremely fierce. The outcome was uncertain until the Mexicans once again withdrew in the middle of the campaign and moved south. U.S. casualties were about seven hundred while Mexican losses totaled about eighteen hundred. After Buena Vista, no fighting occurred in northern Mexico for the rest of the war. Taylor remained in command of a small force there to ensure control until he returned to the United States in November 1847.

Taylor's victory in northeastern Mexico helped make him a popular hero and presidential candidate in 1848. The war was going well for the United States. U.S. armies were winning spectacular victories against great odds. They had occupied almost all of northern Mexico.

The Mexican-American War

CHAPTER 4

The United States Conquers Mexico

While looking for a way to end the war, President Polk was also concerned that General Taylor would make a very popular Whig presidential candidate in 1848. Polk did not want Taylor to become too popular and win the election. Polk decided to try a new strategy for winning the war with a different general. Polk's choice for a new army commander was General Winfield Scott. Scott planned to land on the east coast of Mexico at Vera Cruz. From there, he would march west and attack the Mexican capital of Mexico City. Polk hoped that the Mexicans would surrender if the United States occupied their capital.

The Invasion of Mexico

In March 1847, Scott and fourteen thousand soldiers landed at Vera Cruz. The city had a natural harbor

▼ On September 17, 1847, General Winfield Scott led his troops into Mexico City to oversee the surrender of the Mexican army by General Santa Anna, as illustrated in this contemporary lithograph.

Winfield Scott (1786–1866)

The great American soldier Winfield Scott fought bravely in the War of 1812 and rose through the ranks from a colonel to a general.

Scott was at the center of all U.S. military activities from the War of 1812 to the Civil War. In 1841, Scott was appointed supreme commander of the U.S. Army. The success of his daring Mexican campaign made him a national hero. In 1852, the Whig Party chose Scott to run for president, but he was defeated by **Democrat** Franklin Pierce.

Fast Fact

An elderly Mexican citizen who watched the American flag being raised over Mexican territory said, "That flag has been my ruin. I came from Spain…and was sent into Louisiana; that flag came and I then went to Florida; in a few years the same flag came, and I then came to this place expecting never to be disturbed by it again. But there it is—the same flag, the same people."

and was one of Mexico's largest cities on the Gulf of Mexico. After an eighteen-day siege and a three-day bombardment, Scott captured the city. He then set out across Mexico.

The campaign was one of the most brilliant in U.S. military history. Scott's troops advanced 260 miles (418 km) across the hostile Mexican countryside. At every battle, the Americans were outnumbered and on the offensive. Yet they suffered fewer casualties than the Mexicans, who had the easier job of defending mountain passes and cities. At no time did Mexico, a nation of seven million people, ever unite to face the invaders. In addition, the average Mexican soldier was a landless peasant while his officer was usually a wealthy landowner. This social gap resulted in poor morale in the Mexican army. Many Mexican soldiers disliked and distrusted their officers.

The battle of Cerro Gordo, fought April 17–18, 1847, was the most important battle of the campaign. At a mountain pass near Jalapa, about 50 miles (80 km) inland and 200 miles (322 km) from Mexico City, nine thousand Americans met thirteen thousand Mexican troops. The Mexicans occupied the high ground blocking the way to Mexico City. The Americans tried to get around the Mexicans by scrambling up the mountainsides. After bitter hand-to-hand fighting, Scott's men forced the Mexicans to flee. The Americans captured three thousand prisoners and a great deal of military equipment and supplies.

The Attack on Mexico City

After the Battle of Cerro Gordo, the American troops continued to move westward. Increasing sickness forced the army to rest in the city of Puebla, about 150 miles (241 km) from Mexico City, for three months. Scott and Santa Anna tried and failed to agree to a peace treaty. When no treaty was produced, the Americans continued their march on Mexico City. In fierce fighting outside the capital, they attacked the fortress at Contreras and routed a large Mexican force at Churubusco, both on August 20, 1847. On that single day, Santa Anna suffered four thousand casualties out of twenty-five thousand men, while Scott only lost one thousand of ten thousand. The Americans took three thousand prisoners including eight generals, two of them former presidents of Mexico.

By early September, sickness had reduced Scott's force to six thousand. Nonetheless, he decided to attack the Mexican capital, a city of more than one hundred thousand inhabitants. On September 13, an American force led by General John Quitman occupied the supposedly unconquerable fortress of Chapultepec, the key to the defense of Mexico City. U.S. troops entered Mexico City the next day and remained there until a peace treaty was signed.

Doniphan's March

During the Mexican-American War, Missouri native Alexander Doniphan led one of the most famous expeditions in U.S. military history. When the war began, Doniphan, serving as brigadier general of Missouri's militia of eight hundred volunteers, marched to Santa Fe. His troops then occupied the city of Chihuahua in northern Mexico and began yet another long march to join forces with Zachary Taylor in late May. They traveled down the Rio Grande, sailed for New Orleans, and returned to Missouri. Doniphan's men journeyed 3,600 miles (5,792 km) with almost no loss of life under difficult conditions.

◀ On his march westward toward the Mexican capital of Mexico City, General Winfield Scott met fierce opposition from Santa Anna's forces in Cerro Gordo, a town nestled in a 10,000-foot (3,050-meter) mountain pass 60 miles (97 km) inland from Vera Cruz. U.S. troops emerged from the battle victorious when army engineers found a hidden route through the mountains, enabling the U.S. soldiers to take the enemy by surprise.

CHAPTER 5

A Soldier's Life

When the Mexican-American War began, the regular U.S. Army had less than eight thousand men. Once the war began, Congress passed a law that allowed President Polk to ask for fifty thousand volunteers to serve for twelve months.

The response was overwhelming. More than two hundred thousand men responded to the call for volunteers. In Tennessee, more than thirty thousand men rushed to enlist. In Ohio three thousand men enlisted in three weeks. There were so many eager young recruits that thousands had to be turned down and sent back home.

In the end, about one hundred thousand Americans served in the armed forces during the Mexican-American War. About seventy-five thousand joined volunteer organizations raised by the states. The rest served in the regular army, navy, or marines.

Life in Camp

The average U.S. soldier was a young man in his twenties. He probably grew up on a farm and joined the army for adventure and glory. Instead, he found only boredom,

▼ This illustration is representative of people in towns all over the country as they gathered to read about the record number of men volunteering to fight for the United States in the Mexican-American War. In this image, African American slaves also listen to news about the war, which will eventually affect the institution of slavery in the United States.

discomfort, and disease. In letters home, U.S. soldiers complained about the food, their officers, the weather, and the character of Mexicans.

The battles of the Mexican-American War took up a very small part of a soldier's life. Soldiers spent most of their time drilling and waiting in camp. Augustus Ehinger, a soldier in the Second Illinois Regiment, remembered, "Every morning at 3 A.M. the reveille is sounded; every man must be in line for inspection of arms. An hour afterwards, we cook our breakfast, eat, and take down our tents, pack and be on the march. This is the rule for every day."

New Weapons

The average Mexican soldier carried an old **flintlock musket** manufactured in England. A musket was a gun with a long barrel that was held on the shoulder. It was loaded at the muzzle, the open end of the gun where the bullet came out. They were called flint-locks because when the trigger was pulled, a sharp piece of flint struck a piece of steel and the spark fired the gun. Flintlocks were difficult to handle and slow to load.

By the 1840s, these flintlocks were out of style in the United States. Instead, some troops began using more reliable percussion-cap muskets. By the end of the Mexican-American War, the two U.S. armories had manufactured almost one hundred thousand new percussion-cap firearms.

No matter how they fired, muskets were effective only when fired together in a big group. A musket was not very accurate, and its range was only about 100 yards (91 meters). Ulysses Grant, a young soldier in the war, later recalled in his memoirs, "At the distance of a few hundred yards a man might fire at you all day without your finding out about it."

▲ Soldiers who fought in street battles during the Mexican-American War used new weapons such as revolvers and rifles, rather than muskets. Muskets, which were effective only when fired in a group, were more suited to battlefields where many organized troops fired in unison.

Army Life

Soldiers always have time to complain about army food. An Illinois soldier in the Mexican-American War was very bitter when describing the food that he and his fellow soldiers were eating: "Starvation is the cry here. Our fare is truly bad enough. We have very fat, rusty side meat, a kind of hard, square bread sent us in barrels...together with coffee.... I can hardly manage to get enough down to preserve me and am somewhat lean just for want of something good to eat."

Fast Fact

About sixty-seven hundred U.S. soldiers deserted during the Mexican-American War.

Soldiers in the Mexican-American War often used a bayonet in close-range fighting.

Another new weapon was the **revolver**. A revolver is a type of handgun usually measuring less than 18 inches (46 centimeters) long and designed to be held and fired with one hand. Samuel Colt had invented this new type of handgun in 1835, but no one wanted to buy it until the U.S. government ordered one thousand revolvers during the Mexican-American War. The revolver was a huge success, and Colt became one of the largest manufacturers in the country.

Very few U.S. soldiers carried a **rifle**. A rifle was similar to a musket except that the barrel was "rifled," or grooved. This rifling gave a bullet spin, similar to the spiral action on a thrown football, which made the weapon much more accurate than a musket. Unfortunately, rifles were slower to load than muskets and were much more likely to jam, misfire, or even blow up in the shooter's face. Some percussion-cap rifles, known as Mississippi rifles, however, were used in the Mexican-American War. This weapon gained its name from its performance in the hands of Jefferson Davis's Mississippi Regiment. Before setting out for Mexico, Davis daringly requested one thousand percussion rifles and managed to have his entire regiment armed with the virtually untried gun. The new rifle performed well enough, but the army did not adopt it until the 1850s.

"Nearly All Who Take Sick Die"

The death rate for the young American men serving in Mexico was ten times greater than the rate for the general population of the United States. Only two thousand, however, of the thirteen thousand U.S. soldiers and sailors who died in the Mexican-American War were killed in battle. Yellow fever, malaria,

The Mexican-American War

measles, diarrhea, and dysentery caused thousands of deaths. One young soldier from Tennessee wrote to his father, "Nearly all who take sick die."

Women and the War

Most American women supported the Mexican-American War. If a soldier was married, his wife had to run the farm and take care of the family while he was gone. As volunteer companies formed, local women began making uniforms, tents, and the company flag. Some women served in the army by cooking food or doing the laundry.

Once the U.S. soldiers were in Mexico, Mexican women worked for the conquering army. In Santa Fe, in 1850, more than three-quarters of Mexican women named "laundress," "seamstress," or "domestic" as their job. Mexican women were usually paid less than Americans were for the same job or work.

Many lonely U.S. soldiers in Mexico struck up relationships with Mexican women whom they met at dances known as fandangos. Other soldiers waited anxiously for mail from loved ones at home. Despite all the U.S. victories, the Mexican-American War lasted longer than anyone expected.

Those women's organizations opposing the Mexican-American War felt that the United States had no right to take over by force lands held by other nations. Women played a key role in many peace groups, such as the American Peace Society and the League of Universal Brotherhood. In 1846, Jane Swisshelm published a series of "war letters" attacking the war against Mexico. She claimed that Southern slaveholders and Northern Democrats supported the war in order to expand slavery.

Jane Swisshelm (1815–1884)

Jane Swisshelm, born in Pittsburgh, Pennsylvania, lost her father at the age of eight. Jane helped support the family by lace making. At fourteen, she became a schoolteacher and later, at the age of twenty-one, married James Swisshelm and moved to Louisville, Kentucky. There she helped slaves who had run away from their masters and a life of bondage.

In 1848, Jane Swisshelm established her own antislavery newspaper in Pittsburgh. She also used the newspaper to support women's rights. The *New York Tribune,* an important newspaper, paid her to contribute a weekly article. In 1850, Swisshelm became the first woman to sit in the U.S. Senate press gallery.

In the 1850s, Swisshelm moved to Minnesota and began another newspaper. A proslavery mob destroyed her printing presses. When the Civil War began, she sold her newspaper and worked as a nurse for the Union army. After the war, Swisshelm retired to Pennsylvania, where she wrote her autobiography, *Half a Century.* She died on July 22, 1884.

CHAPTER 6

The Treaty of Guadalupe Hidalgo

▼ *General Zachary Taylor led twenty-three hundred American troops at the Battle of Palo Alto, where, even though outnumbered by six thousand Mexican soldiers, they were victorious. The Mexican army lost about one hundred soldiers, compared to the U.S. loss of fifty-three. An oil painting by Nathaniel Currier dramatizes the battle.*

In 1847, President Polk told Congress that, if the United States won the war, he wanted all of Texas to the Rio Grande line. He also wanted to take New Mexico and California.

Those who opposed taking a large amount of land from Mexico held a strange mixture of differing positions. They included most Whigs and many Northern Democrats who feared the expansion of slavery. White Southerners, however, were not keen on taking too much Mexican territory either. They did not want to add large numbers of blacks and so-called mixed-race Mexicans to the U.S. population.

In April 1847, Polk sent Nicholas Trist, a former ambassador to Cuba, to make a peace treaty with Mexico.

The Mexicans did not want to give up more land than Texas and a small part of California. The United States, however, refused to return thousands of acres of conquered territory to Mexico. In late 1847, Polk added eighteen thousand soldiers to Scott's army in order to fortify the conquered territories and ordered Trist to return to the United States. The United States now occupied major Mexican cities such as Mexico City, Vera Cruz, Tampico, Cuernavaca, Pachuca, and Toluca. The United States had not conquered all of Mexico, but the Mexicans were not in a strong position to negotiate.

A Treaty at Last

By the time Trist received Polk's orders to return to the United States, Santa Anna had been overthrown again. Faced with Mexican anger over his failure to defend the country, Santa Anna resigned the Mexican presidency in September and fled the country in October. The new Mexican leader, Manuel de la Peña y Peña, was eager to negotiate a treaty so the U.S. troops would leave Mexican soil. With Scott's support, Trist ignored Polk's order to return. Instead, he stayed to write the Treaty of Guadalupe Hidalgo, signed on February 2, 1848.

The Treaty of Guadalupe Hidalgo approved U.S. claims to Texas and set the state's boundary at the Rio Grande. Mexico also gave California and New Mexico (which contained the future states of Nevada, Utah, and Arizona) to the United States. These 530,000 square miles (1,372,700 sq km) made up more than one-third of Mexico's territory, although they contained very little of its population. The new lands increased the size of the United States by more than 20 percent. In exchange, the United States paid Mexico $15 million for California and New Mexico.

This land transfer meant that the United States absorbed the region's 150,000 Indians and 75,000 Spanish-speaking residents. According to the treaty, these new Americans were supposed to be guaranteed civil and political rights as well as their rights to their land.

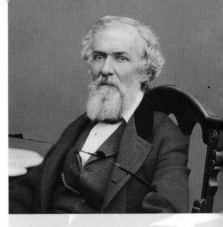

Nicholas Trist (1800-1874)

Nicholas Trist, pictured above, was born in Charlottesville, Virginia, in 1800. He was a cadet at West Point and studied law under Thomas Jefferson, whose granddaughter Trist later married. Trist served as a private secretary to Andrew Jackson during his presidency and later as U.S. representative to Cuba. Trist's knowledge of Latin American ways and his fluency in Spanish made him an ideal choice to negotiate a treaty with Mexico. Trist's refusal to heed his president's orders to return to the United States in the midst of treaty negotiations made him one of the most controversial figures in politics at the time. His uncompromising belief that Mexico's full surrender of military forces and territory was the only way to justify the costs of the Mexican-American War led to the 1848 Treaty of Guadalupe Hidalgo. Trist's decision to disobey the president and stand by his principles greatly benefited the United States but cost him a future in politics.

Ratification

President Polk was furious with Trist for refusing to follow orders. He had to admit, however, that the Treaty of Guadalupe Hidalgo agreed with his original instructions.

The U.S. Senate voted to ratify the treaty by a 38 to 14 vote on March 10, 1848. In May, the Mexican congress also consented. On June 12, 1848, after a nine-month occupation by the United States, the flag of Mexico replaced the American flag at the national palace in Mexico City. California, New Mexico, and Texas now belonged to the United States. Between twenty-five thousand and fifty thousand Mexicans had died in vain defending their homeland.

▼ The map of territory ceded to the United States by Mexico after the war (colored in green) includes California and what would eventually become the states of Utah, Nevada, Colorado, Arizona, and New Mexico.

Polk's Victory

James Polk was not shy about boasting of his accomplishments. He wrote, "The acquisition of California and New Mexico, the settlement of the Oregon boundary and the annexation of Texas, extending to the Rio Grande, are results which, combined, are of greater consequence and will add more to the strength and wealth of the nation than any which have preceded them since the adoption of the Constitution."

Utah and the Mormons

The Mormon Church, or the Church of Jesus Christ of Latter-day Saints, began in upstate New York in 1923. Persecution forced the **Mormons** to move to Ohio, Missouri, and then to Illinois. In 1844, a mob in Nauvo, Illinois, murdered Joseph Smith, the founder of the religion, and Mormon leaders decided they needed to move outside the United States to escape discrimination. In 1845, the first Mormons arrived in Utah, then a remote and generally ignored Mexican territory. Two years later, Brigham Young announced that they had found their promised land. In 1848, the Mormons learned that they had not left the United States after all. Utah had passed into U.S. hands as a result of the Mexican-American War.

The Mexican-American War

The California Gold Rush

The acquisition of California proved incredibly lucky for the United States in a way that no one had ever considered. In 1848, gold was discovered along the American River at Sutter's Mill in the Sacramento Valley, starting the **gold rush.**

Americans caught "gold fever." Thousands of people left their families, quit their jobs, sold their farms, or deserted the army and ran off to California. In 1845, fewer than one thousand Americans lived in California; by 1850, there were more than one hundred thousand. The population of the village of San Francisco exploded from one thousand people in 1848 to thirty-five thousand in 1850.

The Fall of the Californios

The discovery of gold in California was an unexpected bonus of the Mexican-American War for the United States. California became the new population center of the western coast while Oregon lost importance. The declining fur trade was not nearly as profitable as gold, and San Francisco had a better harbor than Seattle or Portland.

The conquest of California by the United States was a disaster for Californios. The Treaty of Guadalupe Hidalgo was supposed to protect the legal rights of the Mexicans now living in the United States. After the gold rush, however, the Californios became a small minority of the population. Although Californios had lived on their lands for generations, most Americans considered them "foreigners." Americans settled illegally on their ranches without permission. Sometimes they used the courts to make unfair claims on the Californios' property. By 1860, 90 percent of the Mexican residents of the region that had been northern Mexico had lost their lands or properties.

Mariano Guadalupe Vallejo (1808–1890)

Mariano Vallejo was born to a wealthy Californio family in Monterey. He joined the Mexican army at fifteen and rose to become the military commander of northern California. After the Mexican-American War, Vallejo was one of eight Californios to serve in California's constitutional convention of 1849. He was then elected to the first California state senate.

Unfortunately, the war caused massive damage to Vallejo's estates. Lawsuits took away almost all his land. By the time of his death, Vallejo led a modest life on a small ranch.

The Treaty of Guadalupe Hidalgo

CHAPTER 7

The Road to Civil War

Although the Mexican-American War cost the United States about $100 million, the result of the war was that American wealth and power expanded. The harbors of San Francisco and San Diego opened the door to U.S. trade with Asia. The rich farmland of California would eventually help feed the nation.

Zachary Taylor and the Election of 1848

The issue of slavery in the new territories dominated the presidential election of 1848. James Polk decided not to run and died only three months after leaving office. In his place the Democrats nominated Lewis Cass from Michigan. Cass believed that the people of the territories should decide the question of slavery for themselves. According to Cass, Congress had no power to interfere.

The Whigs (led by their Southern members) nominated General Zachary Taylor, the Mexican-American War hero. Taylor had taken few stands on any issues. Most white Southerners supported him

▼ An 1830 print made from an engraving was used by abolitionists to campaign against slavery in the new territories gained by defeating Mexico in the war.

because he was one of the largest slave owners in Louisiana. White Southerners also believed in a concept known as **states' rights**. They argued that the Tenth Amendment to the U.S. Constitution guaranteed that certain legal rights remained with individual states and not the national government. White Southerners claimed that the right to own a slave was one of those rights and that each individual state should decide for itself whether slavery was legal or illegal. In this way, slave owners hoped to protect themselves against some future time when the national government would make slavery illegal. Many white Southerners distrusted Lewis Cass because he was from the North. They felt safe with the slave-owning general.

Taylor won the election. His success as a war hero in the Mexican-American War was enough to gain the goodwill and support of the majority of the U.S. voting population. Slave owners, however, had guessed incorrectly. Taylor, a lifelong military man, was a stubborn believer in the power of the national government. To the shock of many white Southerners, Taylor had little sympathy for slave owners' appeals to states' rights.

"Free Soil" for the New Territories

The Mexican-American War split the Whig Party. Northern Whigs who were opposed to slavery drifted into a new political party called the Free Soil Party. Southern Whigs either joined the Democratic Party or dropped out of politics.

The Free Soil Party wanted slavery forbidden in any territory taken from Mexico. Free Soilers did not support the abolition of slavery. Instead, they believed that the national government had the constitutional right to stop the spread of slavery into the territories taken from Mexico.

"On Civil Disobedience"

Henry David Thoreau, pictured above, the author of *Walden,* went to jail in 1846 rather than pay taxes that would support the Mexican-American War. In an essay called "On Civil Disobedience," he explained that a person had a moral right to oppose a government that was acting immorally. "On Civil Disobedience" later influenced Mohandas Gandhi's efforts to remove the British from India in the first half of the twentieth century. Martin Luther King Jr. and other activists used Thoreau's model of civil disobedience in the black civil rights movement in the 1950s and 1960s.

Frederick Douglass (1818–1895)

Frederick Douglass, pictured above, spent his youth as a slave on the Eastern Shore of Maryland. In 1838, he ran away to New York City. In 1841, Douglass made his first antislavery speech to a white audience. He was a powerful and convincing speaker. He attacked both slavery in the South and racial discrimination in the North. In 1845, he published his best-selling *Narrative of the Life of Frederick Douglass.*

During the Civil War, Douglass pressed Abraham Lincoln to support the end of slavery. Douglass also helped the War Department recruit black soldiers. In 1888, Douglass was appointed U.S. minister to Haiti.

The Compromise of 1850

In 1849, the United States consisted of fifteen states where slavery was legal and fifteen states where slavery was illegal. That balance was threatened when California applied for admission to the United States as a free state. California's admission would give the antislavery states an advantage in the U.S. Senate, where each state has two senators.

White Southerners said they would support California's admission as a free state only if the national government guaranteed that slavery would always be legal in the United States.

Debate in Congress was very bitter, and a civil war threatened to break out. President Taylor surprised everyone by supporting California's admission as a free state. Taylor opposed any compromise, but before he could effectively govern on the issue, he died of food poisoning. Taylor's death made Vice President Millard Fillmore president. His support for a compromise led to a temporary solution.

The so-called Compromise of 1850 allowed California to enter the United States as a free state. In exchange, Northerners agreed to support the Fugitive Slave Law. This law required the police, even in free states, to capture and return runaway slaves to their owners. The other territories taken from Mexico could decide for themselves if they would allow slavery.

A Major Cause of the Civil War

Neither the North nor the South were completely happy with the Compromise of 1850. The issue of slavery in the western territories became harder and harder to compromise on as the 1850s passed. In 1854, people in the North formed the

The Mexican-American War

Republican Party. The Republicans strongly believed that there should be no slavery in the territories taken from Mexico.

In 1860, the Republican candidate, Abraham Lincoln, was elected president of the United States. As a Republican, Lincoln believed that slavery should not expand to the West. However, in his first speech in 1861, he specifically promised, "I have no purpose, directly or indirectly, to interfere with the institution of slavery in the States where it exists." Eleven Southern states did not believe him. They decided to **secede** from the union of the United States and form their own country, called the **Confederate States of America**. President Lincoln strongly opposed breaking up the United States. In 1861, the Civil War began when Southern rebels attacked Fort Sumter, a Union fort outside Charleston, South Carolina.

The attack on Fort Sumter took place only thirteen years after the end of the Mexican-American War. The division between North and South over the expansion of slavery into the new territories taken from Mexico was one of the most important causes leading to the Civil War.

▼ *Victory in the Mexican-American War set in motion a national debate over the institution of slavery, which would result in an attack on the Union's Fort Sumter by Southern rebels in 1861.*

TIME LINE

1816	Spanish government sets Texas's southern border at the Nueces River, 130 miles (209 km) northeast of the Rio Grande.
1821	Mexico wins its independence from Spain.
	Moses Austin receives a land grant in Texas from the Mexican government.
1835	Texas Revolt begins.
1836	Texans win independence at Battle of San Jacinto.
1837	Texas becomes independent country known as the Republic of Texas.
1841	Population of Oregon multiplies. By 1845, six thousand Americans will live there.
1844	James Polk defeats Henry Clay in extremely close U.S. presidential election.
1845	Newspaperman John O'Sullivan first uses the term "manifest destiny."
	U.S. Congress admits Texas as twenty-eighth state of the United States.
	The United States claims the Rio Grande as the southern border of Texas.
	Mormons arrive in Utah.
1846	U.S. Senate ratifies Oregon Compromise treaty. Polk orders U.S. soldiers into disputed area in Texas between the Rio Grande and the Nueces River.
	Americans rout Mexicans at Resaca de la Palma; Mexican-American War begins.
	U.S. soldiers conquer New Mexico and California; the Bear Flag Republic is formed.
	Antonio López de Santa Anna returns to Mexico, takes command of the Mexican army, and is declared president of Mexico.
1847	Taos Revolt put down in Santa Fe.
	The United States wins Battle of Buena Vista.
	Winfield Scott's forces land in Vera Cruz; march 260 miles (418 km) to Mexico City.
	U.S. forces under Scott win battles of Cerro Gordo, Churubusco, and Chapultepec.
	U.S. forces occupy Mexico City.
1848	Treaty of Guadalupe Hidalgo ends Mexican-American War; Mexico surrenders one-third of its territory.
1849	California gold rush begins.
1850	Zachary Taylor dies in office; succeeded by Millard Fillmore.
	Compromise of 1850 allows California to enter the United States as a free state.
1860	Ninety percent of Mexican residents no longer own land in California.
	Abraham Lincoln is elected president.
1861	The Civil War begins.

GLOSSARY

abolitionists people who favored ending slavery in the United States before 1865

ambassador an authorized representative of one's country

annex to join or to add

Californios people of Spanish descent in California

canal a waterway that people build to improve transportation or navigation

Confederate States of America a republic formed in February 1861 and composed of the eleven Southern states that seceded from the United States in order to preserve slavery and states' rights. The Confederacy was dissolved in 1865 after being defeated in the Civil War.

Democrat member of the Democratic Party

Electoral College a group of electors chosen by the voters to elect the president and vice president of the United States. The number of electors given to each state is based on that state's population.

expansionism a nation's policy of enlarging its territory either by peaceful means or by conquest

flintlock a type of firearm in which a flint fixed in the hammer produces a spark that ignites a charge

gold rush a large migration of people to a newly discovered gold field

latitude the distance north or south of the earth's equator, measured in degrees on a map

Mormon a member of the church that follows the teachings of Joseph Smith, who published the Book of Mormon in 1830

musket a muzzle-loading shoulder gun with a long barrel

nationalism devotion to the interests or culture of a particular nation

proviso a condition

revolver a pistol having a revolving cylinder with several bullet chambers that may be fired in succession

rifle a firearm with spiral grooves within the gun barrel, meant to be fired from the shoulder

secede to withdraw formally from membership in an organization or union

siege the surrounding and blockading of a city, town, or fortress by an army attempting to capture it

social reform a movement that tries to improve certain aspects of a society

states' rights a political position that limits the power of the federal government over the states and extends law making powers to the states to the greatest possible degree

Tejanos people of Spanish or Mexican descent born in Texas

Whigs members of the Whig Party, a nineteenth-century political party formed to oppose the Democrats

FOR FURTHER INFORMATION

Books

Bardhan-Quallen, Sudipta. *The Mexican-American War.* Detroit: Blackbirch Press, 2005.

Carey, Charles W. *The Mexican War: "Mr. Polk's War."* Berkeley Heights, NJ: Enslow, 2002.

Haberle, Susan. *The Mexican War, 1846–1848.* Mankato, MN: Bridgestone Books, 2003.

Howes, Kelly King. *Mexican-American War.* Detroit: UXL, 2003.

Kendall, George Wilkins. *Dispatches from the Mexican War.* Ed. Lawrence Cress. Norman: University of Oklahoma Press, 1999.

Sonneborn, Liz. *The Mexican-American War: A Primary Source History of the Expansion of the Western Lands of the United States.* New York: Rosen, 2005.

Web Sites

Invasión Yanqui: The Mexican War.
www.humanities-interactive.org/invasionyanqui/

The Mexican War.
www.latinamericanstudies.org/mexico.htm

U.S.-Mexican War, 1846–1848. KERA-TV Dallas/Fort Worth for PBS.
www.pbs.org/kera/usmexicanwar/

The U.S. Mexican War. Descendants of the Mexican War.
www.dmwv.org/mexwar/mexwar1.htm

Publisher's note to educators and parents: Our editors have carefully reviewed these Web sites to ensure that they are suitable for children. Many Web sites change frequently, however, and we cannot guarantee that a site's future contents will continue to meet our high standards of quality and educational value. Be advised that children should be closely supervised whenever they access the Internet.

INDEX

About the Authors

Jon Sterngass and Matthew Kachur have collaborated on a variety of books for children. Jon is a freelance writer with a Ph.D. in history from City University of New York. He is the author of *First Resorts: Pursuing Pleasure at Saratoga Springs, Newport, and Coney Island.* He lives in Saratoga Springs, New York, with his wife and two sons. Matthew lives in Eastchester, New York, with his two children.